1979

A Rain of Rites

For Runu

A Rain of Rites

Jayanta Mahapatra

The University of Georgia Press, Athens

Acknowledgments

The author and the publisher gratefully acknowledge permission to reprint the following poems which originally appeared in the periodicals noted: "Dawn," "Village," "A Rain of Rites," "A Rain," "The Whorehouse in a Calcutta Street," "The Face," and "Now When We Think of Compromise," *Poetry;* "These Women," *Meanjin Quarterly;* "A Missing Person," "Myth," "Silence," "Listening to a Prayer," "On the Bank of the Ganges," "Evening," "Moving," and "An Old Country," *Critical Quarterly;* "Samsāra," *Northwest Review;* "Listening," "Summer," "Sunburst," "I Hear My Fingers Sadly Touching an Ivory Key," "Hands," and "Of Armour," *Chicago Review;* "Ceremony," "The Sentence," "Four Rain Poems" and "Dawn at Puri," *Sewanee Review* (copyright 1976 by the *Sewanee Review*); "Indian Summer Poem," *Times Literary Supplement;* "The Bare Arms in Packing Cases" and "The Desert Under the Breath," *Malahat Review;* "Somewhere, My Man," *Queen's Quarterly;* "This Stranger, My Daughter," *Southern Poetry Review;* "The Tattooed Taste," *Opinion;* "Appearances," *Quest;* "A Dead Boy," *Saint Andrews Review;* "Girl Shopping in a Department Store," *Quetzal;* "Idyll," *Mundus Artium.*

Library of Congress Catalog Card Number: 75-41831
International Standard Book Number: 0-8203-0397-6 (cloth); 0-8203-0396-8 (paper)
The University of Georgia Press, Athens 30602

Contents

Dawn

Out of the dark it whirls back
into a darkly mysterious house.

Is it the earth within?
Does it keep us waking, give brief respite?

Like a hard crossword puzzle
it sets riddles crowding against one another:

the thunders trailing around hatchet-faced banana leaves,
a front gate limp with dew,

the acid sounds of a distant temple bell,
the wet silent night of a crow that hangs in the first sun.

Is the dawn only a way through such strange terrain?
The frenzy of noise, which a silence recalls

through companions lost, things suddenly found?
There is a dawn which travels alone,

without the effort of creation, without puzzle.
It stands simply, framed in the door, white in the air:

an Indian woman, piled up to her silences,
waiting for what the world will only let her do.

Village

The survivors pretend to be sleeping.
Not all voices, the earth,
the sentimental place they thought they'd left behind.
Carefully I cross
the palm-trunk bridge over the irrigation-canal,
and the grave-green waters flow on, limping.
Doesn't its laziness deceive your eyes?
The peepul-tree-silence on the bleak burning ground?
Beside the low mud walls of a hut,
Radha, in the hurt-filled light
of an early November sunset,
in the sterile sameness
of the grass-lined call of the children.

There yet the mourning doves
fluttering out of the tall plumes of bamboo,
those first virtues
that make a country count,
while a freezing sense of inutility sits
on the dark brown throat of a woman
where the scarlet mark of the gods
had swept over through the years,
a suffering, subtle spirit.
Can the rows of lost souls out there in the trees
fill you?
And does one know too much of things of the world?

2

To the vermilion-smeared, whored stone
and bleary-eyed listless cattle of a slumbering land,
she shyly bows to a world of her own
(was everything past only a lie?)
the evening sun indifferently passing by,
leaving behind on her body
the awe of shadow,
before another shadow creeps upon her skin,
hesitant, intangible, real,
as over the stone,
as in a womb where love perhaps had never been.

Old Palaces

I

In a limbo of things that accept the past
the blood grows softer, glossier, in the shadows.
Here the string goes lax
that holds the sky, fluxes of the will, the vague far places.
The distance opens and closes the palms of my hands.

II

Trying to go back
fulfills fantasy, patterns of childhood, the clear bondage.
Yet perhaps the soul, dispiriting enemy
inside my own age, tribe and tongue,
gives proof enough against annihilation.

III

What can remain to meaning here
deadens gestures, footfalls, faces of our nature.
Disused things yield themselves to our
arrivals and departures, sun and rain, relationships:
cold reminders of gods I had hoped to escape forever.

IV

In high ceilinged rooms the lofty uncommon light
frees things from one another, each object
on its own darkness, definitive, as though charged
with the voice of a bird no longer there, sucked into the skies.
The century's smell floats in the air like an act of treachery.

V

If I hesitate for dreams to come, the memories
of this light, the quartz staircase of flight;
to invoke the last glance of a lotus-footed princess
who fluttered across the now-deserted corridors of stone,
isn't it only my soul staggering on the meaningless
blue of the sky the bird carried away on its wings?

VI

The rot and dust pick up such casual afternoons,
sifting their aura of power across the senses;
what souls are proof against the knowledge of where they live?
What brings us face to face, across the palace's
golden light locked inside that secret lens?
Not the thought that succeeds in pushing the darkness,
                          evil and ugliness out of my life.

These Women

Red chillies spread on a reed mat.
Deeper in our skins
the women.

Where are things called homes
sticky with toil; need after need
tempts the fates to touch them,
trap the homely embarrassed hurt.

Year after year
like onions and herbs hung out to dry
their hearts heavy
the quiet too long.

What do they live for
beyond the veils of innocent prayer
the climb up and down the holy stairs?

They seed, though.

They close their eyes everywhere
to that end
airing the poise of a flower.

A Missing Person

In the darkened room
a woman
cannot find her reflection in the mirror

waiting as usual
at the edge of sleep

In her hands she holds
the oil lamp
whose drunken yellow flames
know where her lonely body hides

Samsāra

In a sky shaking itself
from the long burning rains,
the first grasses of cirrus.

And autumn's dream: the year's
newly resurrected gods
move out of their sleep.

Somewhere
a fair Brahman priest
waits haughtily by the temple doors.

A prayer falls,
to wander around
the deserted targets of the soul.

Offerings of marigolds, fruit and shaven hair
stare like terrified men;
the slow stone surges to flame.

And a man begins to begin again
in the centre of this past,
and sees no end of it.

"Samsāra": *Samsāra* literally means "wandering" and represents the trans-
migration of the human soul through endless reincarnations in human
or animal form as a result of good or bad *karma* (conduct).

Five Indian Songs

I

A thousand years answer my ochre heart
through the ends of my dead grandmother's hair.
Stars and my grandfather
are anchored in this darkness
patterned without passion,
and made for a reverence to last.

II

In the ponds of dirty water
the sun beats slowly
like an exhausted sparrow.
The air smells of sick, mortal children.
Stone feels warm as a pillow.
Why do I think of endless, ancient wisdom?

III

The childhood never leaves us.
A fire warms only those
who have their arms to trust.

IV

These brick-batted roads of violence
which go on breathing after dark,
I can feel the air that wounds.

V

Schools, too, rest on silence.
What is childhood then?
Like lepers dragging legs
louder than words,
all dead
the simple meat.

A Rain of Rites

Sometimes a rain comes
slowly across the sky, that turns
upon its grey cloud, breaking away into light
before it reaches its objective.

The rain I have known and traded all this life
is thrown like kelp on the beach.
Like some shape of conscience I cannot look at,
a malignant purpose in a nun's eye.

Who was the last man on earth,
to whom the cold cloud brought the blood to his face?
Numbly I climb to the mountain-tops of ours
where my own soul quivers on the edge of answers.

Which still, stale air sits on an angel's wings?
What holds my rain so it's hard to overcome?

A Rain

I

If it is a game one invents.
If I know of the endless desert.

II

The clear, wise eyes of water, running.
The look on the other side of life.

Not how or where I want it,
nor this earth. Just an evidence,

or truth, knowing the body
is warm enough for its feeling.

III

Watching behind the wall, I see
it play over people, piled up to their silences.

It creates an impression of vastness.
It quietly opens a door.

If I am growing like earth or stone
I will not hear the sad weeping words.

IV

If it is a game one has made in childhood,
there will be no word to hide in.

The Exile

Land's distance.
Walking where the mouldy village
rests rawly against the hills,
the charred ruins of sun.

Corpses smoulder past my night.
The wind hurls the ashes of the present,
to settle in the corners of my skin.

I walk back,
drugged,
between old, ill parents.
Around me, my squalid town,
the long-haired priest of Kāli
who still packs stolen jasmines
into a goddess's morning eye;
a father's symbols:
the door I am afraid to close.

It is an exile.
Between good and evil
where I need the sting of death.
Where a country's ghosts
pull my eyes toward birth.
It is an obscure relative I've never seen.
Every time.
The duty of carrying my inconsequences
in Father's house.
It is there in my son's eyes up the tree.

Listening

A far sleep rests in these people,
that is near, and all. The look
every father wears: not to know the deep need,
the simple salt, the body's lying call.

Every season here droops
into its shabby nest. At the touch of stone
the immensity becomes your own: gods, fathers, sons,
binding into earth, becoming one and centre.

Every man, every beast,
trapped, deaf in his own sleep.
Only the wind you hear, that scallops
the silence of a whole birth, speaking

from the skies where nothing moves:
the horizon black, motionless; the old hills
which define memory, stars of myth whose surfaces
sling silence. And yet what weaves into sleep is not false.

And there's no point in checking the time.
No point in crossing that ceremonial river
of a hundred thousand lies.
You merely wait, listening, pinned to the stone.

Summer

Not yet.

Under the mango tree
the cold ash
of a deserted fire.

Who needs the future?

A ten-year old girl
combs her mother's hair,
where crows of rivalries
are quietly nesting.

The home will never
be hers.

In a corner of her mind
a living green mango
drops softly to earth.

Ceremony

A strange spirit sculpts the trees;
the strangeness plays in the breeze, an ancient voice,
                              is the world to the mind.
I close my eyes, feeling the million prayers
sitting on the villages across the land of my father;
a warm memory, a cry behind the deodars.
Years have broken time into small fragments of light and
        shadow;
elsewhere a hawk swoops to its deep experience of hope,
a large group of stony women in front of a shrine
silently sit out the whole day waiting to be cured,
of their own will, their supernatural eye,
                              to see the sad nature of themselves
return their stares of dry, drab weeds.
And in the trees a chatter of monkeys.
With what brief magic can a little life waken?
What is there in ceremony, in a ritual's deeply hidden meaning?
The familiar words are rude like roots, and out of place,
hanging like history in which one's sky stumbles.
In the world it is always I who come back
to myself, that far flower of thought;
the sacred cold books flash with star pyres.
                              And a small guilt veins
the leaves of my touch, fills my naked ears
like a spirit. Any cult here, triumphs for ever.
The indistinguishable bodies stretched on the dusty earth
hone the ceremony to a hard glow,
a spasm pulls me from the depths of sunken sleep,
across those empty cages of time which measure that road.

Main Temple Street, Puri

Children, brown as earth, continue to laugh
at cripples and mating mongrels.
Nobody ever bothers about them.

The temple points to unending rhythm.

On the dusty street the colour of shorn scalp
there are things moving all the time
and yet nothing seems to go away from sight.

Injuries drowsy with the heat.

And that sky there,
claimed by inviolable authority,
hanging on to its crutches of silence.

"Main Temple Street, Puri": Puri is perhaps the holiest place of pilgrimage
in the whole of India. Situated on the eastern coast, overlooking the
Bay of Bengal, it is famed for its ancient temple of Jagannath (literally,
Lord of the Universe). Religious belief draws thousands of pilgrims to
Puri throughout the year, especially at the time of the annual car festival,
when the Lord of the Universe is taken outside the temple for his
symbolic tour of the world to study the state of mankind.

The Whorehouse in a Calcutta Street

Walk right in. It is yours.
Where the house smiles wryly into the lighted street.
Think of the women
you wished to know and haven't.
The faces in the posters, the public hoardings.
And who are all *there* together,
those who put the house there
for the startled eye to fall upon,
where pasts join, and where they part.

The sacred hollow courtyard
that harbours the promise of a great conspiracy.
Yet nothing you do
makes a heresy of that house.
Are you ashamed to believe you're in this?
Then think of the secret moonlight of the women
left behind their false chatter,
perhaps their reminding themselves
of looked-after children and of home:
the shooting stars in the eager darkness of return.

Dream children, dark, superfluous;
you miss them in the house's dark spaces, how can't you?
Even the women don't wear them—
like jewels or precious stones at the throat;
the faint feeling deep at a woman's centre
that brings back the discarded things:
the little turnings of blood
at the far edge of the rainbow.

You fall back against her in the dumb light,
trying to learn something more about women—
while she does what she thinks proper to please you,
the sweet, the little things, the imagined;
until the statue of the man within
you've believed in throughout the years
comes back to you, a disobeying toy—
and the walls you wanted to pull down
mirror only of things mortal, and passing by:
like a girl holding on to your wide wilderness,
as though it were real, as though the renewing voice
tore the membrane of your half-woken mind
when, like a door, her words close behind:
"Hurry, will you? Let me go,"
and her lonely breath thrashed against your kind.

The Sentence

It isn't that one is imagining things.
It isn't that the night locks you in,
hangs you from its sleepless whispers.

      Nor a god

nipping in and out of secret pasts,
that lines your feet in stone.

      It is

your father's distant night under your bone?
Listening. The small close stream he built
twisted like a cry under his hands,

     a ghost

curled cold inside your belly.
Act like a stranger while you live.
How does the crow fly?
And will the swift clouds stop, turn for you,
ever?

      Behind

the locked door you're waiting for things,

     those reasons:

something that lives in the brittle reeds of your veins
something that urges the relentless trees

     to whisper of their years.

A Twilight Poem

Indian dusk: cool half-lit eyes
stir the troubled soul to design.

A needed belief,
in the sullen throat of ruins.

If now, an old man's face
appears on the darkened ledge,
the whewing of the wind
fills one with dense exile.

You know of night, and what a seed,
a dead grandfather's face is like.

Across the shadows,
a water-buffalo wallows in the marsh's ooze;
a naked boy calls:
his voice stumbling on his own body
drowsy with the day-long cries of forbidding crows.

Appearances

A humble light spins under the old banyan.
Crouched down beside the village elders
a student from the city cringes of habit.

A million years pass between sunrise and sunset.
It is difficult to distinguish one from the other.
Under the tree a dead leaf stares stiffly as a scholar.

Passing by, I hear the rustling of leaves
that sounds the same everywhere:
the lonely drone of a stupid fairy tale, where once

some holy curse changed a woman to stone.
The beginning of a country under the tree's jumbled shade
answers from the end,

a dream of smiling children licking
the aging faces around; the birth for which I search
is the death that scatters my family among the boughs.

Myth

Years drift sluggishly through the air,
is a chanting, the long years, an incense.
Face upon face returns to the barbed horizons
of the foggy temple; here lies
a crumpled leaf, a filthy scarlet flower
out of placeless pasts, on the motionless stairs.
                                        Old brassy bells
moulded by memories, dark, unfulfilled,
to make the year come back again—
a recurring prayer.
                            The stairs seem endless,
lifelong,
            and those peaks too, Annapurna, Dhaulagiri;
uncertain, impressive as gods.
                                        I dare not go
into the dark, dank sanctum
                where the myth shifts
swiftly from hand to hand, eye to eye.
                                The dried, sacrificed
flowers smile at me. I have become;
                                a diamond in my eye.
Vague grieving years pit against the distant peaks
like a dying butterfly
                                as a bearded, saffron-robed
man asks me, firmly:
                                Are you a Hindoo?

"Myth": Annapurna and Dhaulagiri are two of the many snow-capped
peaks in the Himalayan range. Supposed to be the abode of the gods,
the awe-inspiring mountains of the Himalayas also contain the source
of the holy river, Gangā.

22

Four Rain Poems

I

In the rain that sails vast spaces
toward the season's end, as a day dies
from the depths of mouthless time,
all movement broken, a drunk, on the winds;
my face is a full white moon
pressed onto the paper-dry surface of dead water.
Thus I approach the boundary between
the voices I make and their drooping echoes,
facing those secrets lost in one's own creation,
now to fold slowly, or rise and fall in turn,
in that inner kingdom of consciousness
which moves each torture of memory into the flesh.

II

Behind me lie inexhaustible worlds.
Through the window I see the submerged sun
slumped in a medley of grave new ash and bone,
mysterious looking boats on the river's edge,
the noises of charred minds of the past, the stirred stale air.
They are menfolk returning from a cremation
drowsy and rebellious to memory,
their tired mouths lying about the need to themselves,
as they let the rain take over once more,
the waters of thoughts moving along beds
of gravel and grass into an even sleep of blood.

III

Drifting across old scars, like a walk
in familiar country, simply celebrates
the abyss of voiceless rain, justifies nothing.
To have the amazement that is a symbol
of what one left, and to return to a condition
for reality: do I know what really is my loss,
do I know what I mean when I say this
while the remembered rain beats against my walls?
This is where the flushed face of unrest
lies waiting for its resolution: to be someone again,
as a window awakens in its strange surge of light,
making magic, like eyes. This lie has no poem.

IV

All night I have waited for the rain to end,
the forbidden memories ringing, compelling
footfalls among the ruins, the day's last sun smoking
in unending fields soaked in innocence.
It is the beginning of a voyage that is over,
a weary voice that will not speak or be heard.
Where is that absence which pushed an icy rope
down my throat, so close my heart could have touched it?
It is a world gone, out of hand, one I cannot recognize,
that draws everything to a close.
Its water rubs softly on my mind;
this water, all the stars' silence, talking to a child.

A Dead Boy

My opaqueness, out of timid thought,
cuts him off. His angel waits
across the tired watercourse.

The day, the year backing away,
a point of reference. How do you go on,
except when you involve the already lost,
in an attitude determined
by the cautious rustle of another hand
against the walls of the moon,
or the whisper of somebody's years
on the slender eye of a sob?

At times this is a paper boat
memory survives to launch.
And there is a smile on the waterface
that will not anchor to yesterday's dawn;
I see the terror stretched
across other smiles
trying to turn their smile back on me.

25

Moving

Drummers on an autumn day,
rain hammering
on the deep stillness of the valley.

The ten-armed clay Durga
framed in a mythic past,
carried slowly by twenty-four tired men.

Moving surrounds us.

A group of temple Brahmans
singing, the tar
quietly melting along the lane.

Dumb silence of a god's curved eye,
directed like a pilgrimage.

Silence

I have read the silence
that dances across the land at dawn.

I have watched it grow
from a small lonely window.

It hurts.
The hundred thousand eyes.

When I try to get over it
it creeps into my bed like a furtive child.

Is it really the waiting I've known?
Words clinging to me like a trick?

Nobody can help me
if I pull the covers over it.

Was it not on the inside,
walking down ahead of me in the morning?

Dawn at Puri

Endless crow noises.
A skull on the holy sands
tilts its empty country towards hunger.

White-clad widowed women
past the centres of their lives
are waiting to enter the Great Temple.

Their austere eyes
stare like those caught in a net,
hanging by the dawn's shining strands of faith.

The frail early light catches
ruined, leprous shells leaning against one another,
a mass of crouched faces without names,

and suddenly breaks out of my hide
into the smoky blaze of a sullen solitary pyre
that fills my aging mother:

her last wish to be cremated here
twisting uncertainly like light
on the shifting sands.

"Dawn at Puri": It is the wish of every pious Hindu to be cremated
at Puri. *Swargadwāra* (Gateway to Heaven) is the name of that part
of the long sea-beach where the funeral pyres go on burning.

Listening to a Prayer

Stone cuts deep

A bell trembles,
touched by the pain
of countless people

Across the temple square,
the wind
that settles on my shoulders
has nowhere to go:
neither a silence
nor an answer

Sunburst

"At the sunburst in the music of their loving"

Richard Murphy

An old fear, the wild flight,
the exploding air
as the foot of propriety slips again.

A common happening, an ordinary day.
It is ten a.m., and schoolgirls
in white frocks and red waistbands are going by.
Autumn leans on the still damp land;
broad-winged hawks go wheeling in strong sunshine.

Huddled close, the friendly crowd watches,
half the street dissolved to speechless breeze.
A black humped bull rides the cow:
two gods copulating on the warm tar,
the morning closed,
the grass throbbing, cruelly ablaze.

The great body of the cow gropes for breath,
a little dribble breaks; taut on her tethered rope
her deep eyes wait in her puzzled knowing
for the rhythm to die; as the man holding on
to the rope coaxes her softly
by name: half woman, half goddess. . . .

Possible, rigid, two shy twelve year olds
glance surreptitiously, then turn their heads away.
It is only human mirrors which shape
an embarrassed scene. Their own hushed bodies
amaze them. Lost in respectability's ruse,
they stare at the road, learning to close their eyes,
to hold their keen pride.

People watch the bull withdraw, staggering a little.
The owner walks his impregnated cow along.
The countryside is buoyed up
in a warm gust of wind.
A queer, haunted kind of dream spins
in the vast sunburst:
a public intimacy,
part growing up, part sacred, most part lust.

Along the mildewed magic bank,
stone-eyed trees furred by vermilion
stare savagely like beasts.

The song of a lone Ganga boatman
stumbles across lofty silences.
Pious bathers crowd the riverside steps.

It could be
that the old blind flow
creates a field of force across the mind;
their faces blank and waxen, alive in a dumb impulse,
drawing of touch to be appeased by mystery.
Is it death which moves the earth? Or birth?

I half-wake from a doze. It is only the wind,
blowing over the water, harsh fire,
that plucks the withered sanskrit flowers on my breath;
while the river lies
with the sullen dignity of an abandoned doll,
used, abused by delinquent children.

And I know I am alone.
Tonight I can remember the lost mornings.
A hawk cries in the gloom:
a purpose on the air, not yet fulfilled.
To be whole, to know how the water lies.

"On the Bank of the Ganges": Throughout the ages the Ganges (Gangā)
has been considered to be India's most sacred and venerated river. For
about 450 million Hindus, a bath in its waters is supposed to cleanse
and purify the bather from his or her sins. Gangā is *the* Mother, the
life-blood of Indian civilization and culture.

Girl Shopping in a Department Store

Her mouth stops talking.
In this pattern
nobody believes in (watch the children),
she covers herself also in glass.

A spell. And takes off her eyes.
The echoes of sad light
spill out the silence in the glass.

All because of honorable nights shut inside.
People rush in and out of themselves,
talking sheepishly to new things.

Girl smiles into the wide window.
For no reason.
Her conspiracy has not yet begun.
There is no reason.
Her smile looks back,
starts to eat her up through the glass.

A Tree

In my room the day neither wakes nor sleeps.
On my desk a pin falls in the middle of a breath.

Outside I see the wind come over to the mango tree.
It is Monday morning week across the push of green.

Something has come into me without my knowing it.
Something (through the days) I've been powerless to stop.

Here, as we touch hands, answer one another's smiles,
what can we learn from those we do not see?

The sky that rests its cloud of blindness on the tree,
a belief placed in a leaf to catch the light.

All day and all night I am moved by myself;
only the tree that is there,
the axes of seasons in a derelict eye.

Indian Summer Poem

Over the soughing of the sombre wind
priests chant louder than ever:
the mouth of India opens.

Crocodiles move into deeper waters.

Mornings of heated middens
smoke under the sun.

The good wife
lies in my bed
through the long afternoon;
dreaming still, unexhausted
by the deep roar of funeral pyres.

The Ruins

Stone to sand take on the color
through a lens, the flush of life.
I watch a cow pause, urinate:
a softly spoken sound out of the past.

Crossing life, often the tired lines
seem to run under my palms.
Someone talks of a work of art,
looking into its little secret:
chipped fingers, the thin crack
running slant along the brow.
So like a word, its blue wings broken,
palpitating, because one has failed
to understand. Nothing that is whole
speaks of the past. Or lives.
Or can form into a word.

Evening

Dusk, the hard forms of day
melting into the future.
The product of my thoughts
is a voice that never seemed to exist before.
Or is it a poem,
four warm and kindly lines thrown around,
to impress its will on us, an illusion?

Solemn, devoid of day's fretful pallor, of pride,
it is the hour that keeps back the illumined hills,
the dazzling adjectives that carved the sunset
in my pain. Should I bury my face
in the darkness that runs
between breaths,
to conjure up a sleep that doesn't wear any dreams?

I would forget the causes of suffering, mine and others,
to justify my evening's spirit, searching the landscape
for the leaf's green, the stone's ochre,
for what I would not make of myself.
It is obvious that it cannot prevent all that is to happen.
Something stands by the door for which I wait;
like a smell that lingers of a dead cow's entrails
the day's crows have dragged up to the skies.

Idyll

Here, on some slab of common stone,
the blue shadows of worship rest;
a grey owl flies past,
the ends of a sacred verse flutter and disperse.

In the dim oil light
a man looks at the girl he had once married.
The last cart winds down by the hillock beyond.
Earth-grass is tipped with silver in the rain.

Sleep descends, a river calmly overflows its banks.
On the stained stone a small puddle trembles
in the ghost-light of the moon.
Is it the earth that catches its breath?
Or is one there?
Only a shredded prayer-flag keeps twisting in the wind.

And something in a woman's eyes tempts confessions
from her husband as they stretch out to sleep.
A time never lost, rising as a mist, that floats
                                        upon the consciousness;
gnarled old trees charring the flesh, beneath the stars,
the gods casually breezing through the air, among bones.

The Bare Arms in Packing Cases

You enable me to last
because of the thought
that I'm learning to grow

Going beyond the words I know
is difficult, to give everything
for one lifetime
sounds sour and aging

You may speak of consequences
like an equation
You may be a tree or a road
waiting for the last sick crow

At eight o'clock in the evening
you open the door
the false hour falls in me
appears as smoke
and begins to run like water

again because of the thought

A belief
of bodies behind the vacant land
like arranged flower pots reassuring us

This light passing over things
to what length
learning the night which splits each quiet leaf

Ikons

Black ikons:
a museum of symbols
silence the land.

Swale mists
still blot out the hills.

And illusion:
the sacred plant in a Hindoo home,
cow and scabbed stone,
a dark rock of answers and air.

What else can the face of crowds show?

Among them a father stands,
looking around, like a hill.
Then, mumbling to himself,
he touches the *linga* with his forehead,
divine earths closing his eyes, a sightless god;
his charred silence
left from an enormous fire
no one can remember.

"Ikons": The *linga* is the phallic symbol. Of black, polished stone, it is
the object of worship in temples dedicated to Siva, the Destroyer, the
most powerful god of the Hindu trinity.

I Hear My Fingers Sadly Touching An Ivory Key

Swans sink wordlessly to the carpet
miles of polished floors
reach out
for the glass of voices

There are gulls crying everywhere
and glazed green grass
in the park with the swans
folding their cold throats

A man does not mean anything.
But the place.
Sitting on the riverbank throwing pebbles
into the muddy current,
a man becomes the place. .
Even that simple enough thing.

    . . .

                          In familiar mornings
early summer breezes shake the palms.
Things move: bicycles, buses, idling bulls;
a whole religion framed by the land.
A man bathes at sunrise with passion,
plucks some holy flowers,
sits down to worship
motionless on a mat.
He knows his fathers well.
His mind, like the sun,
gently climbs the godly hill of day,
will not touch or reveal

                        the many levels
of himself.

    . . .

Somewhere
a door opens and shuts.
Years elapse quietly behind,

                    like things
people have known all along.
An idle rickshaw-puller gets up,
polishes the thin chromium trappings
with a rag,
spits on the ground

                    and sits down again,
patiently waiting for fares.

    . . .

Each year, in the spring,
the same things drift by:
clouds of silk-cotton seeds, more
naked children, the virus of pox.
Here sits my man
in the doorway of a dunged street,
beside his ailing mother,

                                    her pinched aged face

proudly bearing the irrelevance

                                    of movement.

Here is the hour that will not move.
Is it made up of old stone?
It holds him now as it held his father.
And it watches like an offering
of flowers at the feet of an ikon,
with the past, with true tolerance.

                                . . .

He waits, with his country,

                                    breathing

and that is all.
What use is there,

                                    tearing

a country to bits?
With his body, he loses body,
pales into a place.
Nothing matters,
the river grows,
the hill takes a high face.
This mystic light oozes everywhere,

                                    like sweat.

Absorbing, it eats his mind
slowly around the edges.

43

Hunger

It was hard to believe the flesh was heavy on my back.
The fisherman said: will you have her, carelessly,
trailing his nets and his nerves, as though his words
sanctified the purpose with which he faced himself.
I saw his white bone thrash his eyes.

I followed him across the sprawling sands,
my mind thumping in the flesh's sling.
Hope lay perhaps in burning the house I lived in.
Silence gripped my sleeves; his body clawed
at the froth his old nets had dragged up from the seas.

In the flickering dark his lean-to opened like a wound.
The wind was I, and the days and nights before.
Palm fronds scratched my skin. Inside the shack
an oil lamp splayed the hours bunched to those walls.
Over and over the sticky soot crossed the space of my mind.

I heard him say: my daughter, she's just turned fifteen. . . .
Feel her. I'll be back soon, your bus leaves at nine.
The sky fell on me, and a father's exhausted wile.
Long and lean, her years were cold as rubber.
She opened her wormy legs wide. I felt the hunger there,
the other one, the fish slithering, turning inside.

An Old Country

Dead grandfathers lift their heads and watch.
They will not speak, politely silent, under protest.

All the wounds litter the sky or lie like craters
high up in the mountains, like laughing children.

Looks can embarrass them, even delirious dreams.
At times they cry out in their silence, calling upon
saints and gods, and they keep asking questions.

Why do they go on asking questions?

Anything is better than the strangled pain,
the puttering around the garden's obese flowers,
hands in the soft generous grass, curled
like question marks.

The Desert under the Breath

You'd think the sand is sore
on top of cool sheets
scattered and unslaked

The moon does not seek its place
clearing the sky
for the sob in your face

The roots carry the thrashed thirst
to the end

Stars restlessly clasp
like hands   words of the mind
showing the repulsion
as you push aside the skin
of the body
finding justification

Lonely in the taste of stretched hunger
you'd think the sand is sore
to the end

And the water alive

Hands

Between them
a silence occupies the whole place.

Slowly my body has walked
into deep water.

As a boy I learned to come in
by the back door. Sad
houses now, clean and leaning
against one another, full of sleep.

My old rag elephant is
smothered with small screams.

From the dark surface,
waving like grass—
When the last boat crosses the lake.

Of *Armour*

Each night the scar tissues clang
those distant church clock bells

and you look beyond her
where you've closed the door
afraid to be your hysterical hour

She is where you have followed her
and where her floating panting space
covers up your declivitous time

You could if you would not
press your own skilled ghost
against her tumbled heart
if she only let you be
yourself naked and gaping
hanging on the doorstep without a name

And in the morning lean
your crumbling hurt again
that had to give away stillness in the night

This Stranger, My Daughter

The grafting goes on through my winters
Each season a stratagem for her smile

I watched her grow   doll-head
huge around sparrow-thighs
sprouted to silence

As the world gives me a nudge

My precious golden daughter
looks out through the glass

I nail two damp eyes to the door
And all the while
the waiting draws me down

Drums beating under the earth
tremble her taut skin

There is a sun we know of
There are
the secret spasms to reason

Juices from my daughter's body
are filling the noisy hives

In an impressive map of lime-washed childhood
can one straggle out,
shift the brutal bones of its boundaries?

The Siva linga,
the rhythmic susurrus of chants on wrecks of petals,
the cage suspended in every father's just eyes.

Small patient birds here sing in the drawn-out summer twilight,
then fall silent to the night.
The trembling of dreams is everywhere, like the wind.

When we learned dumbly to grow,
we felt of ourselves abandoned in the wilds, in things not real,
full of the mysterious fog that excites the shadows of the spirit.

Perhaps all the time
you're looking out for the brief lull in the battle
to take a little nap,
to lead the children down the garden path
and restore the breath the living holds,
free the guilt-ridden senses like an afterbirth of life.
And yet does it make any sense anyway?
Or is this an immolation of your uneasiness
on the altar of dream?

You turn around. What is there to explore?
You want to reconnoitre your position.
It is not dawn yet
and something in the dark stirs up a mind.
You remember a boy standing on the horizon
clear and even as glass, like a blank heart, waiting.
Waves of a future like a bell's vague ringing
swirled into you, carrying your body inside,
all innocent, condemned. And then perhaps
you wanted to do something for yourself.

Accepting the absence of you. The few shards
and spirits and bones you haven't been
able to recover down the iron years.
Where you sit, in snide dreaming,
you have your own death.
What is this thing which won't let you sit back,
which you cannot share? Is it
a too true transience that flenses your life
of your own face stranded in that relentless glass?

That's what,
you don't know where you live. Inside.
The sun sleeps somewhere inside your chequered brain,
the darkness bears the conviction of cemeteries.
Then perhaps you turn round suddenly,
seeing him for the first time,
how his accusations search your memory for a beginning,
and your feet move tamely in belief
among your tended plants of paradise.

The Face

I do not dare to see the happiness in it.
Folded in by many thoughts of the mind,
it takes possession of my dark, a powerful god.
The question in my eye never answers itself.

The sky still goes on exploding against it:
the miles of substance my mortality has travelled over;
in a corner of its wish the bones of a child slowly stir,
shaken by a wind that walks in pride among the clouds.

Stranger or intimate, I must carry its voice, the swans
of slumber, with me. Its delicate ivory, I know,
shall destroy me while I live: my hands brooding over
a dead race, the disciplines of ancient tablets of clay.

And yet, the evenings of a silence I've known
endure into the vast night of my face.
There, the warriors still march inside a sticky mist.
What is the thing that owns me? The face

which knows it's doomed, balanced as a precarious sunset?
Or, had I found at last the success in my quiet life,
hanging like a puppet on a string in a pantomime,
indifferent to another life in the faces of others?

The Faces

These faces, unslaked; perhaps ordained,
bleakly wild to the burning ground.
All winds twisting off the storm-centered Bay.
The familiar darkness
climbs out and away from the holy city's sewers,
forming in unexpected places: crevices between prayers,
those hurried mouths that curl their dead tongues to their thirst—
islands of meekness squeezed against the light.

They are martyrs then. If blood turns their years
in their veins, hurts their scapulars on the fierce stone,
they do not reveal the hand that holds the offal.
An existence where flames burn truces in their hands.
A movement of a thousand horizons in the skull.
And fire: the rubbed hands of the future,
blinding the human ground.

Across these faces deserted station platforms sweep by.
They are asleep, haunted by irrelevance, in the things they love.
I listen to their dreams, loaded with skulky shrines,
not understanding them, nor the painful autumns
that sway in the white branches like stalks of bone.
Even my father's face is turned inside out, in which
the gathering dead set themselves into the rush of the world,
the essential ash tightening around my chest
with those arms of creaking, rusty births it bears.

The Tattooed Taste

Night heads downwards across the Indian ocean.
In the cold main road of my rain-smothered town
a man begs for alms, sitting under an old tree
holding his paralysed boy with damp, awkward arms.

Men out of the shadows of dark trees of beliefs,
their principles held out like hands or laughter
going past him, down the old worn steps,
good flaccid fathers
who grow their own vegetables in their gardens,
love their neighbours,
doling out palmfuls of rice on holy Mondays,
the talk of their past days
chained almost, a desire, minds stacked
with sacred ash, looking up, and
heard over the sound of the sea.

Endlessly the amber pearls of light
run along a theatre marquee on the other side of the street,
pulling couples with half-lit eyes inside,
as though possessed, even the boy's broken threads of light.
The astral chariot shines in the neons
of empty-faced women, climbing;
children slumped open, loitering past where they were born,
staring out of their fairy-tale windows
where the wizened wind, sweeping in,
spins high hopes to the ground in silence.

And the man is sitting still, thinking of destiny,
the sea pounding away up the golden beaches at Puri, Calangute
eternity moving hands of sun and gladness
over faces across the sands where
they arc into the water like gulls.

He tells his son
a story of forgotten kingdoms, wars of the just:
a relic of generations
spreading out like a wave
on the sandy beach of his day.
It is the same always,
every dream does its bit
even to men feeling around in the dark
dropping their practised actions
with a proffered hand.

And the man raises *the* little hand to his lips
seeing the feeble smile like the stub of a smoking cigarette
and thinks:
does he know the boy's mind, knowing
that he smiled, his broken body too,
thumping on his own body's battlefield?
His closed clutched hand, his sorrow? What grief is?
And how one is here, as he knows,
rising like the wind to a breeze
toward an understanding by one perhaps who put him there,
then held in its grieved revelation
and seeing his phantom hands melting into the night.

The light of dead mystics laves the night,
the silent upheaval of the river, a way of life;
the holy mists rolling respectably in men's faces
as the man gets up
lifting the boy to his shoulder
without reproach or protest

And sees in the moonlight pulling on
their old ropes of silver
the dark shapes of changing seas
like so many desperate struggles of the dying,
then asks himself over and over again
is he one of them, the dying,
dreaming of how the world should be?

Or the one who knows the time he's waiting for
would never come, and if it came
there'd be no one there, no doors to enter,
no morning, no private tear of pain?
Or is he the truly cursed,
his hand across that dead distance of himself
to love what his silence cannot grasp;
the quivering of diseased gods
only lunging up between his barren fingers:
purposeful daggers that decide,
but will not kill for mercy.

"The Tattooed Taste": Mondays are generally considered sacred in
Orissa, when devout Hindus abstain from taking fish or meat and dole
out alms to beggars and lepers who shuffle from house to house.
    Puri is also a seaside resort like Calangute, near Bombay, on the west
coast of India. Both have wide sprawling beaches and attract numerous
holiday-makers during the summer months.

At times the sunlight loses its fleeting habit
and with simple fingers touches my feet, as though
it was preparing the place, the sombre earths of a rite.
It is then that we fall silent, feeling a tremor through
our empty hands, forbidden colours telling us where
    we want to go.

Far far out, across ten thousand visions, the sun
is a sullen individual of light consigned to the wild white dawn.
It becomes a struggle where we wait, to let it come,
between the beginnings of life and a transgression.
Can our dreams tell what ambiguities our natures
    beg to hold?

We all want to find the man who can rise out of his rite.
And yet we are the ones who'll never let ourselves out,
who hang here and there like decorations on the walls
    of our cries.
Now with my terrible silence I follow the fingers of a conjurer.
I feel the sunlight assess and judge the shapes of our hands.